T0383995

The Little Encyclopedia of
FAIRIES

The Little Encyclopedia of

FAIRIES

An **A-to-Z Guide** to

Fae Magic

Ojo Opanike

Illustrated by Kate Forrester

RUNNING PRESS
PHILADELPHIA

Running Press
Hachette Book Group
1290 Avenue of the Americas, New York, NY 10104
www.runningpress.com
@Running_Press

First Edition: February 2024

Published by Running Press, an imprint of Hachette Book Group, Inc.
The Running Press name and logo are trademarks of Hachette Book Group, Inc.

The Hachette Speakers Bureau provides a wide range of authors for speaking events. To find out more, go to www.hachettespeakersbureau.com or email HachetteSpeakers@hbgusa.com.

Running Press books may be purchased in bulk for business, educational, or promotional use. For more information, please contact your local bookseller or the Hachette Book Group Special Markets Department at Special.Markets@hbgusa.com.

The publisher is not responsible for websites (or their content) that are not owned by the publisher.

Print book cover and interior design by Katie Benezra.
Written by Ojo Opanike.

Library of Congress Cataloging-in-Publication Data
Names: Opanike, Ojo, author. | Forrester, Kate (Illustrator), illustrator.
Title: The little encyclopedia of fairies : an A-to-Z guide to fae magic / Ojo Opanike ; Illustrated by Kate Forrester.
Description: First edition. | Philadelphia : Running Press, 2024. | Includes bibliographical references and index.
Identifiers: LCCN 2023027674 (print) | LCCN 2023027675 (ebook) | ISBN 9780762484836 (hardcover) | ISBN 9780762487387 (ebook)
Subjects: LCSH: Fairies—Encyclopedia. | Folklore—Encyclopedias. | Mythology—Encyclopedias.
Classification: LCC GR549 .O63 2024 (print) | LCC GR549 (ebook) | DDC 398.21—dc23/ eng/20230725
LC record available at https://lccn.loc.gov/2023027674
LC ebook record available at https://lccn.loc.gov/2023027675

ISBNs: 978-0-7624-8483-6 (hardcover), 978-0-7624-8738-7 (ebook)

Printed in the United States of America

LSC-C

Printing 1, 2023

CONTENTS

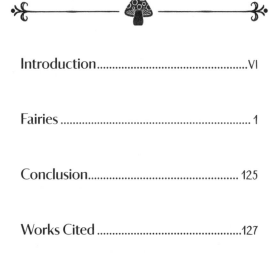

INTRODUCTION

———— 🍄 ————

F airies are possibly the most enduring folk creatures of all time. They feature prominently in
pop culture through fan-favorite characters like
Tinkerbell and Puck. But the concept of typically
small, supernatural beings stretches not just across
time but also across place. The world over, cultures
have converged on this idea that there are unsee-
able forces at play that can (and do) affect our lives.

Whether it's the Alux, a Mayan nature
spirit with the power to call upon rain; or the
Brazilian caipora, who dwell in forests and protect animals from hunters; or Ashinaga and
Tenaga, symbiotic goblins from Japanese folklore, it's clear that fairies (a term interpreted
broadly in this book to include non-Western
fae concepts) are prevalent everywhere. The
similarities across cultures and time periods
are remarkable: The fae beings rounded up in
this book are often miniature or small in stat-
ure, have the ability to shape-shift, and share

an affinity with the natural world; these are just a few of the resemblances you may notice throughout the entries. But there are notable differences, too, especially in the ways that these fairies regard humans. Some enjoy being helpful, offering humans gifts in the form of wisdom or gold or abundant crops. Others are neutral, preferring to live peacefully among one another. Others have a naughty streak and will act according to their own whims, regardless of how their actions affect people.

The breadth and range of creatures collected here proves something essential about us: As people, we are always seeking an explanation for the things we can't control—or the things we can't understand or see. For all those big and small mysteries in life, fairies fill in the gaps. The next time you lose a sock in the dryer or find a twenty-dollar bill between the couch cushions or score tickets to a Beyoncé concert, maybe it was just random dumb luck. Or maybe it was a fairy.

FAIRIES

A

ABATWA

NOT TO BE confused with the real-life, short-statured African tribe known as the Batwa, the mythological Abatwa is the collective name of a group of tiny and elusive hunters in the Zulu territories, home to the largest ethnic group in South Africa. Most of what was recorded initially about the Abatwa from English texts was from the ethnographic

records in Henry Callaway's 1868 monograph *Nursery Tales, Traditions, and Histories of the Zulus.* According to this text, the Abatwa are nomadic and prefer privacy. They prey on large animals, which they kill with poisoned arrows. They waste nothing, leaving no leftovers after consuming their kill. The Abatwa utilize ants to search for hunting grounds and stand on the ant's back, forming a line from head to toe. If they don't find food, they are known to eat the very ants they ride on.

It was said that when they encountered the Abatwa, the Zulu had to be careful not to mention the Abatwa's size because the Abatwa were sensitive to being called small. Even better was if a person regarded an Umutwa (the term for a single Abatwa) as being large. For example, a Zulu hunter who met an Umutwa could say, "Yesterday I saw you by that great lake, but I did not greet you because I was very scared by your great size. So I ran away."

The myth of the Abatwa, as recorded, is the product of European anthropologists who heard about these little people and simply assumed them to be fairies—or equivalent to other tribes, like the pygmies. The story of the Abatwa is complex due to the Zulu term Batwa, used to describe their neighboring tribe.

ACHACHILA

A LARGE GROUP of Indigenous South American people called the Aymara live on the Altiplano plateau, which covers areas that extend from Peru and Bolivia to Argentina and Chile. The Aymara believe in protective spirits called the Achachila, who are said to reside in the mountains and on the plateau. These spirits are tied to specific mountains, such as the Nevado Illimani, Illampu, and Huayna Potosí. Celebrations are held in honor of these spirits through various rituals, like the one in Puerto Acosta, a town near Lake Titicaca, in honor of the Auki Auki, who represents an Achachila in human form.

AGUANE

THE AGUANE ARE female fairies who live in the hills, rivers, and streams of the mountains of northern Italy, the Austrian Alps, and Slovenia. They are beautiful, possess luxurious hair, and can have the hooves of a goat or a horse. An Aguane can also shape-shift to change its form and appearance.

The Aguane are friendly, but humans are advised to ask permission to set foot in their territory because they are known to eat trespassers, especially humans who stir up the mud at the bottom of the riverbeds where they live. However, they are very fond of children and often give them piggyback rides across the river.

AITVARAS

IN SOME BALTIC cultures, when people experience unexpected good fortune, they may hear the phrase "Perhaps you were gifted by an Aitvaras." That phrase originates from Aitvaras, a flying deity and house spirit from Lithuanian folklore. They are considered shape-shifting beings who take on different forms depending on their environment, be it black cats or roosters when indoors, or dragons and serpents with fiery tails when outside. Aitvaras are traditionally associated with immense power and can punish people through actions such as destroying crops with forest fires. They can, however, also aid the oppressed, bringing good luck in the form of grain and money that they take from the wicked. There are many stories in folktales about how to domesticate Aitvaras, some of which include leaving them eggs, milk, honey, and other tasty foods. The name of these beings appeared in the first printed Lithuanian book, *Katekizmo Paprasti Žodžiai* (*The Simple Words of Catechism*) by Martynas Mažvydas. After the advent of Christianity, Aitvaras became mostly associated with theft and evil deeds; however, as the phrase that opens this entry suggests, an association with good fortune persists for these mythical creatures.

ALP-LUACHRA

THE MYTH OF the Alp-luachra is perhaps an evolution from a misapprehension of newts, those semiaquatic salamanders that alternate life between land and sea. In Celtic mythology, the Alp-luachra were known by an Irish expression that means "joint eaters." They were considered invisible fairies who essentially fed on the human body, entering the body cavity by climbing in through the mouth of those who

fell asleep by a stream. From there, they would feast on the essence of the food inside the host, sucking the life force while they continued to grow healthily, increasing in size until they were able to reproduce. This left the human host to suffer, becoming emaciated and always hungry. The lack of evidence for the existence of the Alp-luachra in the body was credited to their ability to avoid detection, even from doctors. There were also stories that suggested an Alp-luachra could be lured out of the body through the smell of extremely savory food. Another purported remedy was eating salty food, then lying by a stream with one's mouth open so that the fairy could jump out on its own.

ALUX

THE MAYAN LEGEND of the Alux, a mischievous little person, has been passed on through the centuries in Mexico. Aluxes are believed to live in the Yucatán Peninsula, birthplace of the Mayan civilization. They are typically invisible but have been known to show themselves when they intend to be malicious or playful. They move quickly and have been said to possess the bodies of animals like iguanas, deer, macaws, or coatis. In some parts of the Yucatán Peninsula, they appear in more frightening forms, including dark shadows or shapes with glowing red eyes.

Aluxes are known for their pranks and can be easily pleased but also angered. They often accost travelers in the jungle to ask for an offering. If the traveler refuses their request, they call other Aluxes and cause chaos for the rest of the traveler's journey. It is advised that humans avoid calling upon Aluxes, as they do not take kindly to being summoned. That's when they take on their most frightening forms.

Apart from jungle pranks, Aluxes were also viewed by Mayan farmers as temporary sources of luck and protection. To invite good tidings, farmers built small homes, or shrines, for the Aluxes to reside in. Farmers believed Aluxes had the power to bring good luck for seven years, ensuring abundant crops, rainfall, and protection of the farm. But when the seven years ended, Aluxes were known to cause mischief again, and farmers would sometimes seal the small house they had built to prevent the Alux from escaping.

ALVEN

IN MIDDLE DUTCH, before the romanticization of elves as tiny winged nature spirits, there existed the monstrous conception of elves in the form of an Alf, a seductive and deceptive being, known for the capacity to manipulate vision. Out of this myth came the Alven, a community of nature spirits that originate from Nordic or Germanic mythology. Some Alven are described as tall, others as tiny, and often they are portrayed in white garments. They burrow in the hillside for shelter and use objects like sieves and eggshells as vehicles for transportation. They create illusions to prank humans and often use their attractiveness to tempt them into misfortune and even insanity. They are also believed to cause nightmares. Some are even considered lewd, seducing humans and swapping their offspring for human babies. The Middle Dutch word *alfsgedrocht*, which means "visual deception," is a product of the Alven myth.

ANHANGÁ

IN BRAZILIAN FOLKLORE, two versions of the myth of the Anhangá (which means "ancient soul") exist. To some native groups, they were viewed as protectors of plants and animals. They were known for not killing or eating animals and for attacking humans who hunted them excessively. The Tupinambá, a collective term for various Indigenous South American groups, held this version of the myth and believed that an Anhangá could take many different forms, including a white deer with fiery eyes. This myth of the Anhangá was used to explain animals that got away from hunters inexplicably, and it was purported that the appearance of the Anhangá was preceded by a whistling sound.

In the second version of the myth of the Anhangá, they were seen as evil shape-shifting beings who were a threat to the dead and the living. In this myth, they were sometimes servants of Jurupari, the god of evil. The contradiction of these myths was either due to the differ-ence between the beliefs of various communities or mis-translations of *Angas,* a term that could mean "souls," leading to the term *vengeful souls,* which could have been mistaken for *Anhangás,* meaning "nature spirits."

ANJANA

ANJANAS ARE SMALL, female fairies from Spanish lore, specifically from the mythologies of Cantabria, an area in northern Spain. They are one of the best-known fairies from the region and serve as mythological foils to the Ojáncanu, which are giant cyclops-like monsters in Cantabrian mythology. In most versions of their myths, Anjanas are beautiful and stand about a half-foot tall, with white skin and soothing voices. In some traditions, they are beings sent by god to do good. They can be seen walking through forests, talking to flowing waters, helping injured animals, healing damaged trees, and helping lost travelers find their way. When called for help, they usually check the summoner's intentions to ensure they are kind before offering their aid. They are said to come out during the spring equinox, scattering roses and dancing while holding hands.

Their name, Anjana, evolved from the word *jana*, which was an old word for witches in the Middle Ages.

AOS SÍ

THE AOS SÍ are powerful fae beings from ancient Irish mythology. Their name translates to "the people of the mounds," but they are often referred to as "the good neighbors" or "the folk" due to people's reverence for their powers. They are believed to have lived in an invisible world, perhaps underground, which coexisted

with the world of humans. An Aos Sí is also known to be both a malevolent and benevolent creature—and a fierce protector of their home. There are numerous stories of the Aos Sí throughout Scotland and Ireland, and many of these myths reference how Norse invaders drove the Scottish inhabitants underground, where they lived in the hills, hence the reference to mounds and subterranean worlds.

APOTAMKIN

DUE TO A brief mention in Stephenie Meyer's Twilight series, the Apotamkin are often presumed to be vampires, yet their legend has nothing to do with the undead. An Apotamkin is a sea monster from the mythology of the Maliseet and Passamaquoddy cultures in North America. They are believed to be giant fanged sea serpents who sometimes drag people, especially children, into the sea and eat them at Passamaquoddy Bay, between the US state of Maine and the Canadian province of New Brunswick. The myth of the Apotamkin has mostly been about teaching children the value of obedience and not venturing off, especially close to the water, without the guidance of their parents. There are, however, versions of the myth of the Apotamkin where they exist as more than sea monsters and are thought to be sometimes benevolent toward humans, saving kids from falling through weak ice.

ASAMANUKPAI

THE LEGENDS OF beings with backward-facing feet exist in various cultures around the world. In West Africa, these legends include that of the tiny Konderong among the Wolof, the Madebele (or Tugubele) of the Senufo, and the bristly haired Dagbani in Ghanaian and Togolese forests. The Asamanukpai, who reside in the Ga Village of Bawyi in the hills marked on maps as Aboaso in modern-day Ghana, are also part of these legends. They are known as little men with feet turned back to front, and the eldest of them have prominent beards. They eat and dance on outcrops of smooth stone, which they polished. This region is also known for disc-shaped thunderstones, which were said to have fallen whole from heaven, with holes formed when caught between the finger and thumb of an Asamanukpa.

Hunters tried to avoid the Aboaso forest because of the myth of Asamanukpai. But if they had to enter, they made an offering of rum, placed on the dancing stone, alongside clean water for the Asamanukpai to wash and play in. When disturbed, the Asamanukpai stoned the offender and led him deeper into the forest, where he would become lost.

Sometimes they took people away to befriend them, taught these chosen ones all they knew, and squeezed the eyes of the captured friend with the juice of a plant that was said to enable the captives to hear their thoughts and see events before they happened. Those subjected to this operation also gained the ability to sing and talk to the Asamanukpai, and they returned to their people to become respected fortune tellers who also gave advice on healing and medicinal matters. They were called Asamanukpatsemei.

In stories among the Osu people, the Asamanukpai are associated not just with the land but also the sea, where they existed in abundance before the much of what has now become Klottey Lagoon dried out. Stories of the Asamanukpai and their human counterparts persisted into the twentieth century and were recorded by people such as anthropologist Margaret Joyce Field.

ASHINAGA AND TENAGA

ASHINAGA AND TENAGA are a pair of yōkai, spirits from Japanese folklore who live in the sea. (The word *yōkai* translates to "strange apparition.") They are known as symbiotic goblins who work together to achieve common goals through their unique physical attributes. Ashinaga is dark-skinned and has long legs that can wade through deep water; meanwhile, Tenaga is the opposite, with fair skin and very long arms for catching fish. With Tenaga on Ashinaga's shoulders, as they are commonly depicted in sculptures, they team up to catch even more fish. They are also described in stories as very strong, using their strength to lift large objects, and a sighting of the pair portends bad weather. The duo is commonly depicted as being from two different locales, a long-legged country and a long-armed country, and paintings of them feature their wild hairstyles.

Ashinaga and Tenaga were first described in the *Wakan Sansai Zue*, an illustrated Japanese encyclopedia from the Edo period, published in 1712 and compiled by Terashima, a doctor from Osaka. Matsura Seizan, an essayist from that time, also recorded a man's anecdotes with Ashinaga.

ASRAI

THE ASRAI ARE aquatic fairies of English origin. Small and slender, they appear young, often looking like teenagers, but have a life span of centuries. Winged creatures who are capable of flight although they fear sunlight, the Asrai also move quickly through water. Their bodies appear translucent, therefore they do not create shadows. An Asrai fairy is associated with freshwater lakes, rivers, and large ponds and will perish if brought to the soil.

Despite their limitations, the Asrai love nature and like to be left alone. They are shy and timid but can also be mischievous. Stories exist of them luring people into the water with promises of jewelry, before drowning them in the deepest parts of the water.

ATTORCROPPES

ATTORCROPPES ARE MALICIOUS fairies of Scottish and Germanic origin whose name means "little poison head," derived from the word *adder*, a venomous viper. They look like small snakes with human arms and legs, enabling them to walk upright. An Attorcroppe is known to be evil but also very curious. Wherever they are found, monstrous snakes are often close by. They love snakes of all types and will often milk their snake friends for poison, which they then put on tiny little spears.

AUKI

THE AUKI ARE mountain-dwelling fairies from the folklore of the Quechua people in Peru. They live in the Andes Mountains, in large houses that look like the ones inhabited by Peruvians. *Quechua people* often refers more generally to those who speak the Quechuan language across Peru, Bolivia, and Ecuador. It was a language spoken primarily by the Incas but was also adopted by their enemies. Today, the Quechua people are mostly associated with

Peru, and here is where an Auki connects to brujos, practitioners of the Indigenous religion, who call upon the Auki to help them cure the sick. A vicuña, a South American camelid, is known as the spirit animal of the Auki.

AZIZA

THE AZIZA ARE creatures from West African Dahomey folklore, in which they were described as tiny people of the forest. They are small and hairy and have wings like butterflies that sometimes grow larger over time. Living among the anthills and silk-cotton trees, the Aziza are known for helping hunters and forest travelers —and for having magical powers to pass on to humans, proffering their wisdom about medicinal plants and fire. The Dahomey people believed that the Aziza were connected to a charm called gbo, which had the power to

protect its owner and hurt their enemies. The term *Aziza* is often used to describe them as a people, but it also refers to a single individual, like in the Jeje oral tradition, in which a pipe-smoking deity shares the same name.

B

BACHNA RACHNA

IN THE FOLKLORE of the Senegalese people, the Bachna Rachna, whose name translates to "good people," are dark-eyed, silver-haired fairies who stand about two feet tall. A Bachna Rachna is known to dance and feast on moonlit nights, even inviting humans to the festivities. The Jaloff people of Gorée Island believed that if the Bachna Rachna needed supplies for their feasts that weren't readily available, they would often steal from people.

BAETATA

A BAETATA IS a being from the folklore of the Tupí-Guaraní-speaking people who live in the Brazilian Amazon basin. The Tupí-Guaraní mythology is a complex system of beliefs and stories that are both ancient and current among the Guaraní people who live in the south-central parts of South America (which span areas of Paraguay and parts of Argentina, Brazil, and Bolivia) and the Tupí people who inhabit the Atlantic coast of Brazil. The legends of the Baetata, who are known as water spirits who have the ability to make rain, are included in this wide-ranging oral tradition. Stories about the Baetata are also very similar to will-o'-the-wisps in their ability to lure humans into the woods, where they can become very lost.

BAKEMONO

BAKEMONO, ALSO KNOWN as obake, are a class of yōkai, which are preternatural creatures in Japanese folklore. They are beings who transform, hence their name, which means "an entity that changes." A bakemono is often referred to as a ghost but is different from a spirit of the dead. Their true form may be an animal—like a fox, badger, or cat—or even a plant. However, they often disguise themselves as humans or in more monstrous forms such as the Hitotsume-kozō, which is a yōkai that looks like a bald-headed child with one eye on its forehead like a cyclops. Many strange apparitions are described as bakemono, too, echoing the definition of the word *yōkai*. Because of the influence of Japanese

culture among Hawaiian people, the term *obake*
is also part of their vocabulary, along with stories of these creatures.

BAKRU

IN MANY PARTS of interior Suriname, when
someone suddenly comes into wealth, their good
fortune is usually said to be the result of a deal
made with the Bakru (also known as Baccoo).
The Bakru are a race of fairies from Paramaribo
in Suriname. They are said to be mischievous and evil fairies who look like children
but are partly made of wood. They have black
skin, black hair, and large eyes with big heads
on small bodies. They always appear in pairs,
one male and the other female. The process of
getting good fortune from a Bakru is said to
involve capturing one and making them a ser-
vant, where an agreement must then be made

to give over one's soul in exchange for whatever riches the Bakru brings. Magicians are believed to be the only ones who can control the Bakru as servants. When the owner of a Bakru dies, they are free to wander and cause mischief.

There are people who believe the Bakru is related to the myth of the àbíkú from the folklore of the Yorùbá people on the West African coast, who live in present-day Nigeria and the Republic of Benin. When a baby dies suddenly, they are said to be àbíkú, and the practice of making wooden statues in honor of the dead babies is said to have evolved into the mythology of the Bakru. There are others who, however, believe that the myth of Mmoatia of the Akan people in present-day Ghana, also along the West African coast, is the origin of the Bakru.

BANSHEE

STORIES ABOUT BANSHEES in Irish folklore
can be traced to the eighth-century myth of
women known as keeners who sang songs to
lament the deaths of people and would sometimes take alcohol as their payment. The term
banshee, which means "a woman of fairyland,"
became widespread in the seventeenth century
to describe versions of the Gaelic mythos. It is
associated mostly with young women, but sometimes with much older women or laundresses
who cleaned blood out of clothes. According
to the myth, a banshee dresses in silver, green,
black, or white and is said to have glowing
eyes. They were also reported to be seen head-
less, carrying a bowl of blood, and naked from
the waist up. Banshees were seldom spotted,
but when they were, it was near riverbanks—
and when not at riverbanks, they were hunting
for young men. The myth of banshees remains

associated with mortality, with legend having it that their wailing warned Irish families of impending death. Although they are not blamed for causing these deaths, some legends speak of banshees who celebrate the demise of people they hate.

BAOBHAN SITH

THE NAME OF the Baobhan Sith is from the Gaelic phrase "woman of the sidhe," or "fairy woman." These beings, known as the white women of the Scottish highlands, are notorious shape-shifters who can take the form of a wolf, a raven, or a hooded crow. A Baobhan Sith also appears in a long green dress that conceals the deer hooves that serve as her feet. They prefer to hunt in packs and are rarely seen alone.

The Baobhan Sith love to seduce men and are often drawn to hunters through the smell of blood. They figure out what the hunter finds attractive, and shape-shift into that form. They begin to dance with their victim until he's entranced, then kill him by slitting his throat with their sharp claws and drink his blood. The Baobhan Sith seem to prefer men who are actively seeking female company, and they are naturally creatures of the dark who are scared of daylight and horses. They can be killed with weapons made of iron, which makes them a kind of precursor to vampires.

BARBEGAZI

THE BARBEGAZI ARE a mysterious type of gnome who reside in the mountainous regions of France and Switzerland. Their name is probably from *barbes glacées*, which means "frozen beards," a reference to their facial hair, which resembles icicles. Their body is covered in hair and

they look like farmers, except for their large feet, which act like snowshoes. They are also much shorter than humans and vary from average to stocky build. The Barbegazi thrive in cold weather and enjoy playing in avalanches, which they often surf down the mountainside. They hibernate through the summer and only become active again in blizzard season. Barbegazi are also known for warning hikers of avalanches by making whistling noises that can be mistaken for the sound of the wind. They are said to help dig out people trapped in snow-falls and herd lost sheep back to their own-ers. Despite this goodwill, their attitude toward humans is uncertain, and they typi-cally remain in the mountains, rarely venturing below the tree line. The myth of the Barbegazi has also been updated to include migration to North America, specifically Roseau County, Minnesota, in the United States, where sight-ings of them have been reported in the winters along the Roseau River.

BARIAUA

A BARIAUA IS a shy, harmless spirit from the folklore of the Tubetube of Melanesia. They disappear if seen by humans and live inside ancient tree trunks. Bariaua borrow boats when they can't make one for themselves—or just steal from fishers. The Tubetube people are native to what is present-day Papua New Guinea, specifically Slade Island, which is part of an archipelago in the Solomon Sea called the Engineer Islands.

BARSTUKAI

A BARSTUKAI IS an ancient Baltic creature, similar to a **kaukas** (see page 79), who lives in nature, in fields and woods and under trees. They are small, some about the size of a finger, and farmers consider them benevolent creatures who protect their barns and guard their grain. There are stories among the Sudovians (western Baltic people also known as Yotvingians) where the Barstukai have feasts in barns, eating bread, cheese, and butter, and drinking beer that farmers leave them overnight. In those stories, if the farmer finds the food intact in the morning, it means the Barstukai did not visit and the harvest will be bad, so they have to prepare accordingly.

BERBEROKA

THE BERBEROKA ARE creatures from the folk-lore of the people from Abra, Apayao, and Ilocos Norte, all northern provinces in the Philippines. They camouflage with forest cover

or rocks, depending on their habitat. They are also able to change their size, so their bodies can contain large amounts of water. They lure their victims by sucking water out of a pond—enough for fish to come to the surface. When the target prey goes for the fish, the Berberoka drowns and swallows them. They can discharge water previously swallowed like the hose of a fire truck. When they make their bodies large, they can also lie in the water to disrupt its flow. Ironically, the Berberoka, despite their obvious monstrosity, are said to suffer from crippling kabourophobia—a fear of crabs, specifically being pinched by them.

BISAN

IN THE PAST, when searching for camphor, the Jakun and Malay people in present-day Malaysia would take a portion of their food and toss it into the jungle before eating as an offering to the bisan, a female spirit who presided over camphor trees and had to be revered before camphor was obtained. They believed the bisan existed in the form of cicadas, which were prominent in the Malaysian jungle. The shrill noises made by these cicadas were indicative of the presence of camphor in trees. Not all trees produced camphor, and the only way to know if a tree had one was after it was cut down, so this belief was part of a larger culture among camphor hunters who trusted in the providential aid of spirits to help them spot the right trees.

The camphor hunters also developed a language called Patang Kapor, which they used exclusively when searching for camphor in the jungle. This language was a combination of Malay and Jakun words. *Patang* means "forbidden" and *Kapor* means "camphor," and for as long as the hunters were in the jungle searching for camphor, they were not allowed to speak any other language but the camphor language to avoid offending the bisan.

BOGGART

BOGGARTS ARE CREATURES of English folk-lore who originated in Celtic lore. Their name is derived from the Welsh word *bwg*, pronounced "boog." Boggarts come into existence from the transformation of a mistreated **brownie** (see next entry), and they are always malicious. Their physical appearance is often described as ugly and hairy, and they have sharp teeth. In their household forms, they are blamed for things like milk going sour and objects disappearing. Their swamp-dwelling counterparts are accused of much more evil doings and are said to be capable of serious harm, such as kidnapping children. Sometimes, an apology or even an act of kindness is considered enough to turn a boggart back into the house goblin it once was. Other times, once the change occurs, it cannot be reversed, and all you can do is leave your house to the boggart. Boggarts make an appearance in J. K. Rowling's Harry Potter books, but their incarnation in that series bears little semblance to the troublemakers of English lore.

BROWNIE

AROUND THE 1600s, it was said that every house had a brownie. They were guardian spirits of dead ancestors, like Lares of Roman mythology. Later, in Scottish lore, brownies became known as spirits or hobgoblins who materialized as small, wizened, brown-skinned, and covered in hair. They lived in trees or abandoned dwellings close to the houses they visited. They were known to be capable of becoming invisible and usually either appeared naked or otherwise dressed in rags. The tradition was for owners of the house to leave some sort of offering on the hearth for the brownies, who came out to perform house chores while those owners slept. The offering could be milk, porridge, treats like cream, or even a small cake, but sour milk was forbidden. Brownies also liked to work with animals and were often friendly to pets. They could, however, be mischievous, and even malicious, turning into **boggarts** (see previous entry) if offended. They began to perform spiteful acts like hiding objects in the house, turning milk sour, and hurting animals. If you tried to clothe a brownie, they could leave you forever.

Brownie lore evolved over time, and in some versions of the stories, their name was derived from their skin tone, which darkened due to exposure to the elements. Speculation also existed about the relation of the myth of brownies to the Covenanters, a Scottish religious movement whose members were driven underground because of their support for a Presbyterian Church of Scotland in the seventeenth century.

BUSCHFRAUEN

THE BUSCHFRAUEN WERE known as the bush-women of Central Europe. They were dwarf-size forest dwellers who were said to have lived in the forests back when they were pristine, before deforestation. They had disheveled golden hair and pendulous bosoms, they dwelled in tree hollows, and they were thought to only go out at night, dancing in the fields to make crops grow. The origin of this myth is very unclear; however, the idea of the Buschfrauen may have come from the nineteenth-century German theatrical performances that represented African people as "bushmen" or "bush-women," a tradition that was rooted in colonial ethnographic practices that featured displays of human beings alongside "curiosities" gathered from the colonies. The most famous example of this was Sarah Baartman (nicknamed Hottentot Venus by the producers of these shows), which in itself arose from the seventeenth-century European use of the word *bushman* in the Cape colony to describe Khoekhoe farmers—pejoratively described as Hottentots—who lost their cattle.

C

CACCAVECCHIA

THE CACCAVECCHIA ARE night elves in Italian folklore who probably originate from Etruscan lore. They are also known as Buffardello and in the Tuscan region are called the Linchetti. A

Caccavecchia is known to climb through holes and enter houses, where it stands on the chest of a sleeping person. They are said to cause nightmares, and people also blame them for strange noises in the house at night. They prefer to stay in barns and do not like disorder.

CAIPORA

THE CAIPORA ARE beings from the mythology of the Tupí-Guaraní people in Brazil. Their name comes from Tupí and means "inhabitant of the forest." They used to be confused for the curupira, another mythical creature who is usually depicted as a boy with red hair and feet turned backward to deceive trackers. A caipora, however, is dark-skinned and small, appearing naked with a long mane. In some regions, they are said to be afraid of the light. In stories, they consider themselves king of the animals and hate hunters who do not respect the rules of fair hunting—that is, tracking and stalking animals humanely. They scare away prey, hide animal tracks, and make hunters lose their way. Some hunters used to make offerings to the caipora for good luck on their hunts. Because legend had it that the caipora liked to smoke cigars, on the fourth night of the week, hunters would leave cigars for them by trees.

COURIL

THE COURIL ARE from the folklore of northwest Brittany, France. They are said to live specifically in the ruins at Tresmalaouen but also in stone circles that can be found in other parts of the region. A Couril looks like a tiny human but with webbed feet. They enjoy dancing and do not like it when humans stumble into their rings. The Couril are said to be related to

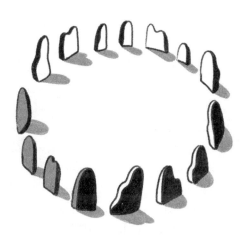

Gorics, a kind of Breton gnome who also loves dancing and dwells in megaliths.

CUARAHU-YARA

CUARAHU-YARA IS A nocturnal creature from Brazilian lore, with stories often told in the Littoral region of Argentina, Paraguay, and southern Brazil. The Cuarahu-Yara is also known as the Pombero and bears similarities to the tales of the Yasí Lateré recounted in Argentina and Paraguay. The Cuarahu-Yara are described as hairy, tall, and wearing large hats. They are known to only appear when their names are spoken. They are characteristically mischievous and associated with benign acts like opening gates and spooking horses or more malicious ones like impregnating women with their hands. Some stories suggest that they could be persuaded to help with household tasks and assist in finding lost items. They are also known to watch after birds and keep kids away from killing them.

D

DJINN

A DJINN (ALSO known as djinni, al-jinn, or jinn) is a shape-shifting spirit from pre-Islamic Arabia. They are amorphous in shape and character and are masters of the elements of nature, with capacities such as making barren land fertile. They have been known to inspire poets by speaking to them, and poets who have experienced this are identified as shā'ir. Because they are mentioned in the Qur'ān, djinns have also been a part of the Islamic religion. They are largely invisible but have been known to possess the body of people who must be exorcised to be free of the djinn. Despite this, it is well established that they are difficult to understand and are considered neither good nor evil. They can

help, and they can hurt; djinns can also fall in love with humans, eat, drink, sleep, and die like humans. Unlike people, however, they live for thousands of years. The myth of djinns became popular around the world from the stories of *The Arabian Nights*, first translated by archeologist Antoine Galland. In those books, djinns were often described as massive creatures with cavernous mouths and wings. They became parts of popular culture through depictions by Barbara Eden in *I Dream of Jeannie* and Robin Williams in Disney's *Aladdin*, which both drew from djinns as described in *The Arabian Nights*.

DOKKAEBI

DOKKAEBIS ARE NATURE spirits from Korean folklore, who manifest as goblin-like creatures. They are described in many forms with multiple faces but frequently wear hanbok,

a colorful Korean formal attire. They inter-
act with humans and often play tricks on
them. A Dokkaebi can give fortunes to people
or punish them for their sins. They are regu-
larly depicted as tricksters but are also capable of good. Dokkaebis are often identified
in types, based on their attributes: A Cham
Dokkaebi is mischievous; a Gae Dokkaebi
is evil; a Gim Seobang Dokkaebi looks like
a farmer and is not smart; a Nat Dokkaebi,
unlike other Dokkaebis, can appear in daylight;
a Go Dokkaebi is good at fighting and using
weapons; Gaksi and Chonggak Dokkaebis are
known to attract and seduce humans; Oenun
Dokkaebis are one-eyed and eat a lot; and an
Oedari Dokkaebi has just one leg.

DUENDE

DUENDES ARE GOBLIN-LIKE creatures from
Iberian, Latin American, and Filipino folklore.
The word *duende* can describe a wide range of fae
beings, and their nature varies from culture to
culture. In Portuguese folklore, they are small
beings who wear big hats and whistle mystical
songs in the forest. In Hispanic cultures, they
are small household beings, about two feet tall,
who do not wear clothes and have long fingers.
They are often depicted as malicious and can
have green skin and red eyes. In Mexico and
the American Southwest, they live in the walls
of houses, especially the bedrooms of young
children. They attempt to clip the toenails of
unkempt children, which can lead to cutting
off the entire toe by mistake. A duende is also
known for taking items from youngsters, but in
some stories they actually play with children. In
Filipino cultures, they live in rocks and caves,

old tree trunks, anthills, and dark untouched parts of homes. They are also known as nuno sa punso (old man of the ground). Light-green duendes were classified as good, while dark-green ones were regarded as bad.

E

EGBÉRÉ

WHEN A CHILD is crying, among the Yorùbá people of southwest Nigeria and the Republic of Benin, they are often told to stop bawling like an Egbéré, a creature from their folklore. These are small creatures who live in remote forests. In stories, Egbéré walk around with a powerful mat, which they take a very long time to carve. Whoever can steal the mat of an Egbéré is often said to become rich because of it. And when the mat is stolen, the Egbéré roams the forest bawling. It is this peculiar cry, which is said to sound like the wailing of a human baby, that gave birth to the saying used in return to chastise crying children.

F

FAR DARRIG

THE FAR DARRIG are creatures with origins in Irish folklore. Their name means "red man." They are known to dress in red clothing, wear red hats, and have long red capes. They are also sometimes called rat boys. A Far Darrig has a reputation as a solitary fairy who is short like a leprechaun, with a pointy nose and ears. They are also depicted with red hair (hence the name)

and sometimes red or gray beards. The Far Darrig are known for their gruesome and mischievous practical jokes. They have skin often covered in dust and go around with burlap sacks big enough to contain people they kidnap on dark nights. They release their captives in a dark room and scare them with growls and animal noises. After having their fun, they let the captives go.

FOMORIAN

THE FOMORIANS ARE a fairy race from Irish mythology believed to have ruled over all of Ireland before the great flood. In some accounts, they are described as personifications of the forces of nature, or one of the first creatures to have settled in Ireland. The origin of the myth of the Fomorians is uncertain. Some of this can be seen in the meaning of their name, which is either derived from *Fo*, which can mean "below," or *mor*, which means "the sea." These etymologies point to the origins of the creatures as either from the underworld or from the sea and are also mixed with the presumed translation of their name as "spirit." In Irish mythology, they were driven off the land and into the sea after going to war with the Tuatha Dé Dannan, a supernatural Irish race whose members were thought to represent the deities. Historically, Fomorians were tall and strong, but they devolved over time after their banishment and became like animals in appearance, each Fomorian distinct from the other.

FOSSEGRIM

FOSSEGRIM IS A male water spirit or troll from
Scandinavian folklore also known as a grim
or a strömkarlen. Fossegrim is always associated with rivers, waterfalls, and millraces. He
plays enchanting songs on the fiddle and can
be convinced to impart his great musical skill
to others. To convince Fossegrim to teach the
fiddle, an offering of food has to be made on
a Thursday evening, but it must be in secret so

people will not attempt to capture him. The offering can be a white male goat turned away from the waterfalls, or smoked mutton stolen from a neighbor four Thursdays in a row. If the goat is too lean or the mutton doesn't have enough meat on the bone, Fossegrim will only teach someone how to tune. If the offering is accepted, he will take the hand of the person who made the offering and run it against the strings until they bleed. After that, the lucky individual will become a great fiddler.

G

GAHONGA

THE GAHONGA IS one of three **Jogah** tribes (see page 73) from the folklore of the North

American Iroquois Confederacy. They live in rocks and near rivers and are said to have the capacity to walk through bedrock. Of the three tribes, the Gahonga have the most interaction with humans. They care about fishing and are often directing the movement of fish, giving them shelter in deep underwater caves, and protecting them from aggressive poaching activities. They are much stronger than their small size would suggest and are also called "stone throwers" because they play a game that involves tossing fairly large rocks back and forth. They can uproot whole trees or grab large stones and hurl them into the river to raise the water level.

GANDAYAH

THE GANDAYAH IS one of the three **Jogah** tribes (see page 73) from Iroquois tradition. They are mostly associated with plants, plant growth, fruits, and grain. They are loved by humans because of their positive association with grain. In springtime, they live in dark places and encourage the earth to bring forth fruit. In the summer, they walk through the fields, ripening fruit and fending off plant diseases that threaten the harvest. They sometimes visit humans in the form of birds. If they arrive as a robin, it's a sign of good things to come. If as an owl, it predicts that a deceitful enemy will approach. If they arrive as a bat, it portends a life-and-death struggle. Each birdlike incarnation is filled with meaning for the humans who encounter them. The Gandayah are fond of strawberries and consider their ripening the beginning of their work.

GANDHARVAS

GANDHARVAS ARE WATER spirits from Hindu, Buddhist, and Jain mythology. They are youthful human-animal hybrids. Some have the face of a bird and the hind legs of a horse or a donkey. A Gandharva is often associated with wilderness and the art of music-making. They haunt remote forests and ponds, and their nature is very capricious. They have intense rivalries with other nature spirits, such as nagas, a race of snakelike deities. They can bestow beautiful singing voices upon girls.

GÖRZONI

GÖRZONI WERE KNOWN as underground folk by the Vends of Lüneburg, a town in northern Germany. Their name was taken from *gora*, which means "hill." They were therefore hill

dwellers, who were known for borrowing bread or baking supplies from people by giving signs invisibly. People often left the bread or utensils for them by the door, and a Görzoni would return the borrowed items in the evenings and often add cakes in thanks.

GREMLINS

DURING WORLD WAR I, English air force pilots called machinery problems the work of "pesky gremlins." They got this term from hearing stories during their childhood about the mythological creatures from the woods of England. The name *gremlin* is said to be from the Old English word *gremia*, which means "to vex." They were known to be mischievous and destructive, and they loved putting things out of order. Wise older women were said to catch them and keep them as pets for their own evil deeds. The 1920

Royal Air Force (RAF) stationed in Malta, the Middle East, and India is credited with coining the larger folklore around gremlins. During World War II, a 1942 article by Hubert Griffith in the *Royal Air Force Journal* talked about gremlins working on plane exteriors and wings. Gremlins, however, still carried the reputation of being troublemakers. In their less harmful state, they became known as Mogwai, remaining benign until they ate food at midnight and turned into gremlins, changing from furry creatures to bat-like ones with sharp teeth and claws. The writer Roald Dahl, who was in the RAF, further popularized the myth of the gremlin in his work, beginning with his first book, titled *The Gremlins.*

H

HALTIJA

A HALTIJA IS a spirit or elf-like creature from Finnish mythology. There are different kinds based on where they live, such as in water, forests, graveyards, or human settlements. There are also personal haltijas, who are protective spirits. Some haltijas are divided into races or folks, called väki, which is based not just on where they live but also on their powers. There are veden väki (water folk), metsän väki (forest folk), naisen väki (womenfolk), kalman väki (death folk), tulen väki (fire folk), vuoren väki (mountain folk), puun väki (wood folk), and raudan väki (iron folk). The powers, attached to women, iron, fire, and graveyards, are for different purposes, which include healing people as well as making them ill, both to help and to hurt.

HEINZELMÄNNCHEN

A HEINZELMÄNNCHEN IS a kobold from the mythology of Cologne, Germany. They are little house gnomes who used to do all the work for the citizens of Cologne at night, including washing their clothes and cleaning their homes. Lore of the origin and disappearance of the Heinzelmännchen says that when the townspeople discovered that their chores were being taken care of, they became lazy and did less and less until all their work was handled by the Heinzelmännchen. A tailor's wife who had been helped tremendously by the Heinzelmännchen wanted to see them in action, so she spread peas on the ground to make the gnomes slip and fall. The gnomes arrived and did slip on the peas, but they escaped and left town. People heard music playing as they departed but couldn't see them. From then on, the citizens of Cologne had to do their own work.

HULDUFÓLK

IN THE FOLKLORE of the Icelandic and Faeroese people, huldufólk are a kind of elf, spirits who live in nature, in a parallel but invisible world. They are big, have black hair, and wear gray clothes. They can make themselves visible at will and take on human forms where the only difference is the convex, rather than concave, philtrum between their nose and upper lip. They live outdoors in mounds, rocks, and cliffs, and Icelanders often say they are part of their dreams—and sometimes their living reality.

In Iceland, belief in the existence of huldufólk is still widespread enough that it

influences infrastructure decisions. The presence of a rock on private property that possibly houses huldufólk is enough to keep that
rock from being destroyed to make way for
new buildings. In stories of unsuccessful road
projects that suffer setbacks and mishaps,
the huldufólk's rock homes on the proposed
routes are blamed. According to a BBC report,
a 2007 study by the University of Iceland suggests that about 62 percent of the country still
believe in the huldufólk. There are cautions
against throwing stones because they may hit a
huldufólk, and it is customary to clean and leave
food for them because they are thought to hold
parties at night.

Some people believe huldufólk change
their abode on New Year's Eve, and they therefore leave candles out on this day to illumi-
nate the way for the migrating huldufólk. And
on Midsummer Eve, it is said that standing at
a crossroad late in the day may bring huldufólk

who can lure the bystander and offer gifts that, if taken, will lead to bad luck.

HULI JING

THE HULI JING is a fox spirit that arose out of ancient Chinese lore. Some myths describe their origins through the story of Daji, the emperor's concubine during the Shang dynasty. Legend has it that Daji was killed by a fox spirit, who then assumed the form of a beautiful woman and took Daji's place beside the emperor. Enamored by his new companion, the emperor neglected his duties in order to spend more time with her. So, the Huli Jing grew in power—and used that power to oppress the country. Eventually, there was an uprising, and the emperor's wife was blamed for the fall of the dynasty. She was killed by the new emperor once he ascended the throne.

Many versions of the fox spirit myth exist in China, but most characterize the Huli Jing as creatures of good or evil, depending on the individual nature of the one encountered. The Huli Jing can create illusions and also appear or disappear willingly. They are shape-shifters, whose forms change as they age. At fifty, the fox gains the ability to morph into a woman. At one hundred, they can change into either a beautiful girl or a wizard. At a thousand years old, they can become celestial foxes.

Although they can be killed, the Huli Jing are often immortal. Sometimes, their fox features show in their human form, like a tail appearing under their dress or fox ears showing on their head. They are scared of dogs and may alter from their human form to their fox form to run away from the canines.

J

JOGAH

THE JOGAH ARE from the folklore of the North American Iroquois Confederacy, which consists of the Seneca, Cayuga, Onondaga, Oneida, and Mohawk people. A Jogah is a small shape-shifter who is considered favorable to humans. The Jogah consist of three distinct tribes: the **Gahonga** (see page 59), **Gandayah** (see page 60), and **Ohdowas** (see page 102).

KAKAMORA

IN THE MOVIE *Moana*, the kakamora are coconut-wearing pirates, a depiction that is based on their existence in Polynesian mythology but does not capture the entirety of their mythos. In Polynesian mythology, a kakamora is a very small and hairy creature who lives in the forest and eats nuts, fruits, and opossums. Their myth continues to exist in remote parts of the Solomon Islands. For example, the author Reverend Charles Fox, who traveled with the Arosi people, wrote of encounters with the kakamora, gleaned from small footprints by the river and half-eaten fish, in his 1924 book *The Threshold of the Pacific*. In 2003, the discovery of eighteen-thousand-year-old human bones on the island of Flores in Indonesia, which archaeologists nicknamed "the Hobbit," revived the myth of the kakamora. Most claims about the kakamora, however, ended in the twentieth century, with the proliferation of guns and the failure of attempts to capture these mythological creatures.

KALLIKANTZAROS

THE KALLIKANTZAROI, ALSO known as karakoncolos, are from the lore of people across Turkey, Bulgaria, Serbia, and Macedonia. Stories about them vary from place to place, but generally, they are described as humanoids who sometimes have animal parts and are predominantly male. The majority are small, have tails, and are occasionally tall and hairy. They are mostly blind and eat frogs, worms, and other creatures. A kallikantzaros can be both mischievous and relatively harmless. And they only appear during the cold parts of the year, for twelve days around the winter solstice.

KAPPA

THE KAPPA, AQUATIC spirits from Japanese folklore, are one of the more popular traditional yōkai in contemporary Japan. Their graphic representations are often found in sushi bars. They are mostly depicted as being the size of a small child with scaly skin that varies from deep green to red or blue. They have a dish-like cavity in their heads that must always hold water. It is said that if the water spills and the dish dries, a kappa may die. The Kappa have bodies built for swimming, with webbed hands and feet and elastic, waterproof skin. They are known as largely solitary in their adult lives but befriend other yōkai and sometimes humans. Younger

Kappa, however, can be found in groups. They are stubborn and honorable and keep all the promises they make.

The Kappa are omnivores, eating anything. However, they like melons, squashes, eggplants, and especially cucumbers. Humans devoted to

them, usually of the Shinto religion—who treat the Kappa as a kind of water god—often leave cucumbers at riverbanks. This is to court the favor of these creatures who are known to help in the irrigation of fields and are often friendly to children. Despite these good deeds, they are also known as potentially violent and mischievous. They love sumo wrestling and really hate cows and horses. Prevailing wisdom is that they can't be bested underwater but can be defeated on land, where they can be tricked to spill the water in their dish, which weakens them. After that, they can be made to swear loyalty to the one who defeats them.

The origins of the myth of the Kappa are vague and not well-known. Some suggest they are based on encounters with animals such as turtles, monkeys, or the now extinct Japanese river otter. These animal influences are often found in graphic depictions of the Kappa.

KAUKAS

THE KAUKAI ARE creatures from Lithuanian mythology in charge of wealth, fertility, and harvest. A single kaukas is small, can be male or female, and has a humanlike body but a triangular head. Kaukai are often dressed in green, blue, or red clothes. They live in forests, woods, and areas with a lot of mushrooms that take their names from the kaukai. If they live in a house, they stay in the dark areas such as basements or cellars, or in dark corners of sheds and barns. They are benevolent spirits in charge of agriculture who bring fortune and good luck. They multiply wheat and hay but never coins or money. They bring skalsa, which increases the supply of objects rather than wealth. The life span of a kaukas is unknown, but it is said that when they die, they go somewhere between birth and death.

KIJIMUNA

THE ISLAND OF Okinawa has its own yōkai, which are distinct from the rest of the Japanese corpus but are nonetheless important to the region. The Kijimuna are an example of such yōkai. They are small wood spirits that are also known as Bunagya (large-headed), who look about four years old and have red hair. The Kijimuna will mimic humans in many ways, including the formation of their communities. Their diet consists of seafood, and they live in trees, especially the gajumaru or banyan tree. A Kijimuna is often an excellent fisher with big catches but loves eating only a fish's left eye before tossing the rest. They also hate octopuses, chickens, and cooking pots. The Kijimuna are known for their mischief and pranks, such as snuffing out lights at night and sitting on people's chests as they sleep. They are, however, said to be friendly with humans and, if encountered, may offer piggybacks across mountains and seas, but hate it when people pass gas on their backs. The story of the Kijimuna, as with other yōkai, is a part of Okinawa culture and is still passed on through the generations.

KIKIMORA

THE KIKIMORA IS a female house spirit from Slavic folklore. They can be helpful or not, depending on how humans who encounter them behave. Stories depict the kikimora with a chicken's beak or a duck's bill. They can also have other parts of an animal's face or body but are often depicted as either older women or beautiful girls. They are fond of any kind of needlework.

Some people say the kikimora can cause nightmares. There are stories of people who had a kikimora sit on their chests while they were sleeping, causing sleep paralysis. Kikimora who marry the house spirit Domoni are always kind to the households where they reside, while the ones from the swamp, who enter the house through keyholes, always cause mischief and sometimes kidnap children. The swamp kikimora visit houses that are very untidy. They can be gotten rid of by keeping the house so clean that they get bored and have nothing to do, which makes them leave.

The myth of the kikimora developed sometime between the eighth and thirteenth centuries, before the advent of Christianity in the Slavic regions. However, belief in these creatures continued, despite the influence of Christianity, because it was a useful myth to establish order and discipline and to explain otherwise inexplicable events. More recently, a kikimora was featured in the television series *The Witcher*, which is based on the fantasy novels by Polish writer Andrzej Sapkowski.

KLABAUTERMANN

KLABAUTERMÄNNERS ARE WATER kobolds
whose name means "to rumble" or "to make a
noise." They are mythical sprites from Germanic
folklore and are usually invisible. They can
show up in human or nonhuman forms. In their
human appearance, they are usually small, about
the size of children. Their legend is most notable among seafarers who are known for assisting
sailors and fishers in the Baltic and North Seas.
Despite their benevolent attributes, they are still
associated with more sinister things that happen
on ships. The version of a Klabautermann associated with mischief is usually more goblin-like
and can doom a ship.

KOBOLD

A KOBOLD IS a sprite from Germanic mythology and present-day German folklore. They are small with scaly skin; long, clawed fingers; reddish-brown or red eyes; and jaws like a crocodile. Some kobolds have wings but are often derided by other kobolds. They are mostly mischievous domestic spirits who help with chores but also hide household tools. They become outraged when not properly fed. Kobolds are aggressive, ingenious, and very skilled at building traps and planning ambushes. Their goal as a race is to conquer as much land as possible, and they put a lot of their industrious energies toward this goal. They entrap their enemies and only attack them physically when they are weakened. Kobolds include Galgemännlein, Heinzelmännchen, and Klabautermänners.

L

LAUMA

LAUMA **IS THE** Latvian term for a guardian
spirit of orphans in eastern Baltic mythology
(also known as laumé in Lithuania). Laumas are
mostly women who appear naked or wear fine
clothing. They are said to have descended from
the sky to the earth because of their compassion
for humans, and there are different myths about
how they arrived on Earth. Laumas live in lakes,
abandoned bathhouses, dense forests, and on
islands. In fact, lots of water pools in Lithuania
are named after fairies. Laumas appear in the
form of animals, such as mares, goats, bears,
and dogs. They also have an anthropomorphic
appearance, which could be the upper body of
a woman, the lower body of a goat, and bird

claws for feet. Laumas are also depicted as half
human, half dog or mare, like centaurs. They
are known to be similar to fairy godmothers
and love animals and humans, especially the
children who they raised. Laumas are, however, known to be dangerous to men, whom they
could tickle to death before eating their bodies. Laumas party out in the meadows on nights

of the full moon or the new moon, singing and dancing and leaving circles (fairy rings) in the grass. They are afraid of tools made of iron, and rainbows are known as their lost ribbons.

LEPRECHAUNS

LEPRECHAUNS ARE SMALL, agile, male fairies from Irish folklore. They are often depicted in old green or red clothing with long ginger-colored or white beards. These solitary creatures are known in stories to guard hidden treasures like pots of gold. They can become helpful spirits but are often mischievous, foul-mouthed, and difficult to catch by people seeking to capture their treasure.

There are many possible origins for leprechauns. Some stories have the source of their myths in the Irish-Celtic god Lugh, originally the god of sun and light before ascending mythologically as the warrior-ruler of ancient Ireland only to fall in recognition with the spread of Christianity over Europe. In this version of the origin, Lugh became relegated to the status of a fairy crafter before becoming a leprechaun, or a fairy goblin. The story of leprechauns is also said to have evolved from the Celtic mythology of ancient small water sprites known as lúchoirp or luchorpáin. These sprites' first appearance in Irish literature was in the *Echtra Fergusa maic Léiti* (*The Adventure of Fergus Son of Léte*), dated around the eighth century CE. Other possible sources are the monsters lupracánaig, who appear in the twelfth-century book *Leabhar Gabhála* (*Book of Invasions*), or the lazy, small-size clúracán, which was known for its similarities to the brownie, or the Far Darrig of Ireland, or the mouros of Celtic Galicia and Asturias in present-day Spain. None of these origins is accepted as the definitive source, but the stories of leprechauns draw from many of them simultaneously.

LUNANTISHEE

IN IRISH FOLKLORE, lunantishees are protectors of the blackthorn tree, a real (but believed to be magical) tree that is a symbol of strength and protection on one side, and trickery if crossed on the other. Historically, on May 11 and November 11, a lunantishee permits no one to cut from the blackthorn. People may leave cake, ale, butter, or milk outside their homes to prevent any mischief from lunantishees, especially if they have blackthorn trees on their property. Sometimes they reward participating people with more blackthorn blessings. The lunantishees are associated with moonstone and are also called moon sidhe, or moon fairies.

MASSERIOL

THE MASSERIOL ARE creatures from northern Italy and the Iberian peninsula. They are usually male and dressed in red and have an elderly face and a laugh that sounds like the neighing of a horse and the bleating of a goat. A Masseriol is usually plump and well-dressed—and occasionally helpful on farms and can tend to livestock and pets. They, however, are very arrogant and think very highly of themselves.

MEMEGWESI

THE MEMEGWESI ARE spirits from the mythologies of the Ojibwe, Cree, Odawa, Algonquin, Innu, Métis, and Menominee people in North America. They are mostly described as hairy, with large heads and child-size bodies, with voices that sound like dragonflies. It is sometimes said that they were created from the bark of trees. Memegwesi are river-dwelling spirits and are considered mostly benign. However, they sometimes become mischievous, stealing things and blowing away canoes. In some Ojibwe traditions, a memegwesi can only be seen by children and medicine people. In other legendry, they can appear to anyone and may help whoever gives them gifts. In Cree and Innu lore, they have narrow faces, and in Menominee, they have no noses. Memegwesi are known to carve symbols on stones and sometimes make small canoes for themselves.

MENEHUNE

MENEHUNE ARE SMALL creatures from Hawaiian mythology. They are very short forest dwellers who are well-known throughout Polynesia and appear in the myths of other Oceanian cultures. They are known as strong and excellent crafters who go out in the dark to build ponds, roads, canoes, walls, and other engineering structures. Menehune try to avoid being seen by humans. If they realize they have been spotted working, they bring their actions to a halt.

The myth of the Menehune is believed to have origins in a human evolutionary ancestor, the *Homo floresiensis,* who lived on Earth at the same time as Neanderthals in Europe and *Homo erectus* in Asia. This and other origin stories about the Menehune are almost exclusively collected in the works of writers such as Thomas George Thrum, the Australian author of *Hawaiian Folk Tales,* published in 1907, who had moved to Oahu in 1853. Many other narratives of Menehune were produced around a similar time line and reproduced in newspapers and journals. Early Native Hawaiians were known to refer to Menehune with the word *kamaʻāina* (child of the land), a term that is now used in reference to residents of the Hawaiian Islands.

MOKUMOKUREN

MOKUMOKUREN ARE YŌKAI from Japanese mythology who live in torn shojis, the Japanese paper screens that serve as sliding walls. Their name means "many eyes" or "continuous eyes." They are inhabitants of haunted houses because when houses are abandoned, and the walls damaged, holes form in the shojis where a mokumokuren may appear. They are mostly harmless, but quite creepy and usually a sign of the presence of other yōkai. The way to get rid of mokumokuren is to patch the holes in the screens.

N

NAGA

NAGAS ARE PART-HUMAN, part-serpent creatures from the myths of Hinduism, Buddhism,
and Jainism. A female naga is called a nagi or
nagini. They are also present in the mythologies
of many South Asian and Southeast Asian cultures, where they appear as either fully human,
fully serpentine, or snakelike from the waist up.
According to the myth, nagas were relegated by
the creator Brahma to the underground because
there were too many on Earth. He told them
to bite anyone evil. They subsequently lived
in an underground kingdom called Naga-loka
or Patala-loka, which was filled with beautiful palaces decorated with precious gems. The
kingdom's king was called Nagawaja. A naga is

known as pretty dangerous, but it also possesses the capacity to be kind to humans. They are associated with bodies of water, including wells, and are also sometimes guardians of treasure.

Artistically, nagas are often represented as hooded cobras with multiple (up to seven) heads, or human beings with hooded snake canopies over their heads. In Buddhism, they are often depicted as door guardians, and in Jainism, the Tirthankara (the twenty-third Parshvanatha—savior—of the religion) is always shown with a canopy of naga hoods above his head.

NINGYO

THE NINGYO ARE mermaids from Japanese folk-lore. They are regarded as being the origina-tors of nightmares rather than seductive sirens. They have very unappealing bodies and sharp claws on their fingers. Their flesh is said to grant eternal life to those who eat it, but it is extremely dangerous to try to catch them. There are stories of entire towns being destroyed by natural disasters because someone brought home a Ningyo.

NISSE

A NISSE, A mythological creature from Scandinavian folklore, is also known as a tomte, tomtenisse, and tonttu. Nisses are associated with the winter solstice and Christmas. They are small but very strong and are often depicted as elderly men with full beards dressed as farmers. A nisse may hide in a house and can help with chores if treated well, for example, when given gifts like a bowl of porridge. If nisses do not receive presents, they can cause mischief and sometimes even wreak havoc like killing livestock. They love animals, especially horses, which they are eager to groom and take care of. Some people say a nisse is also a shape-shifter, skilled in becoming invisible.

NUKU-MAI-TORE

THE NUKU-MAI-TORE ARE spirits from Maori mythology who live in forests. These tree-dwelling spirits are said to spend most of their lives in tight-knit communities. There are many different depictions of their appearance. Some say they have little heads but large chests and waists, while others say they have no head, chest, or waist. There are also stories where their arms and legs are so short that a Nuku-mai-tore seems to have no limbs at all.

NÛÑNË'HI

THE NÛÑNË'HI ARE a race of spirits from Cherokee mythology whose name means "the people who live anywhere." The Cherokee believed they were immortal spirits very different from gods, nature spirits, and ghosts. They are said to have lived in underground houses throughout the Appalachian mountains and were fond of mountain peaks without timber. Hunters often thought they heard them, but when they walked closer to the sound, it would come from a different direction. Lore suggests that a hunter could only see a Nûñnë'hi when it allowed it. In their visible state, they looked, dressed, and spoke just like the Cherokee.

The Nûñnë'hi were fond of music and dancing and were known for being friendly and benevolent toward the Cherokee. They helped those who got lost during the winters and took them into their homes to warm them up before sending them on their way. They also warned the Cherokee of imminent danger, and there are stories of how they helped them during the removal of 1838 when the Cherokee were forced out of their lands to present-day Oklahoma.

NYKR

THE NYKR ARE male water spirits who usually appear in human form, from the folklore of English, German, and Scandinavian people. These shape-shifting spirits play violins

by lakes, storms, or waterfalls and try to lure humans into water. They are malicious in some stories but friendly in others. Sometimes, they are naked by the water, but other times they wear elegant clothing. A Nykr could also appear floating in the water, or as an animal, especially a brook horse. When appearing as a human, the hem of their clothes is always wet.

NYMPHS

NYMPHS ARE GREEK mythological spirits who appear as beautiful young women. They preside over springs, trees, caverns, meadows, and beaches. A nymph can metamorphose into a plant or an animal, and sometimes human women can even be changed into nymphs. They are neither gods nor mortals, but they live much longer than human beings and eat heavenly food. In myths, they are usually lovers of gods

and heroes, or their mothers. They are playful and enjoy frolicking with satyrs. They often
share names with the places where they live.

O

OHDOWAS

OHDOWAS ARE ONE of three types of the
mountain-dwelling **Jogah** (see page 73) from
the folklore of the Iroquois people of North
America. An Ohdowa is a small nature spirit
who controls the underworld and its inhabitant
spirit animals. They exist in folklore to keep
spirit animals from escaping into the light of
the known world.

P

PATUPAIAREHE

THE PATUPAIAREHE ARE beings from the Maori traditions, and they are known to live in forests or misty mountaintops. They are also called Tūrehu or Pakepakehā. They have light skin and red or light-colored hair. A Patupaiarehe is seldom observed and lures people with flute music. They are afraid of light and can only be seen at night or in the mist. They are good at fishing and sometimes teach people magical chants and skills.

PILLYWIGGINS

PILLYWIGGINS ARE HYTER sprites, which are small, elusive fairies with sand-colored skin and green eyes. They have wings and antennae, like insects. Although they are rarely spotted, they can often be heard rustling among leaves and singing. A Pillywiggin won't bother a human with a prank. They live in small, tight-knit communities, which are connected to specific plants or places, and move around in swarms. They cover their bodies with leaves, which help them to travel unnoticed, and are capable of biting and stinging when they swarm to attack. Pillywiggins are clever, resourceful, and very careful with their duties.

PIXIE

PIXIES COME FROM the folklore of southwestern England. They are likely the fairies you are most familiar with, because they are very popular in the West and have received widespread coverage in pop culture over the years. A pixie is a tiny elf-like spirit dressed in green, usually depicted with a youthful face and pointy ears. They are mischievous creatures who are fond of music and love dancing in the moonlight to the songs of frogs and crickets. They love putting out candles, playing with water, and frightening young women. But pixies can also be benevolent. Nature can fall under their dreamy spells, which make plants grow and flowers bloom. They often wear rags but will put on new clothes if gifted. Pixies live underground, sometimes in hollowed tree trunks, and they are very protective of their homes.

PORTUNES

PORTUNES ARE CREATURES from English and French mythology. They are called Neptunes by the French. A portune is helpful, offering support on farms with hard work and also assisting households at night. Late in the day, they often sit in front of fires, cooking frogs over them. They can also be mischievous, and their primary way of showing mischief is by leading horses into ponds at night.

S

SALAMANDERS

IN MEDIEVAL EUROPE, salamanders were considered elemental nature spirits of fire. They were often depicted as lizards, small balls of light, or tongues of fire. A salamander had shape-shifting qualities and was able to increase or reduce its size at will. On rare occasions, they appeared as fairylike beings. Salamanders were said to have taught humans how to make fire and were considered necessary for creating any kind of fire, no matter how small. They were also called to help when fires got out of hand.

THE SEELIE COURT

SEELIE **IN THE** Scots language of the Scottish lowlands means "happy." The Seelie Court is one of the major courts of the fairies associated with benevolence toward humans. The fairy courts are social structures of the fae society that recruit new members, build armies, and have seasonal power. The Seelie Court is known for believing in old fairy traditions and ways of life. It tries to build an orderly fae society that is governed with less chaos and where human servitude is banished. Despite harboring a general good nature toward humans, the Seelie Court can seek revenge when offended. It can also return good favor and prefers not to be indebted to anyone. The Seelie Court fairies are often seen at twilight and sometimes at dawn. And they can become invisible by drinking water or eating a pebble.

Most of what is known about the Seelie
and **Unseelie Courts** (see page 116) is recent.
The courts occur in nineteenth- and twentieth-
century texts, such as Charles Rogers's *Scotland,
Social and Domestic*, published in 1869, and Sir
Walter Scott's 1830 *Letters on Demonology*. There
are also ballads from the fourteenth to seventeenth century that feature the Seelie Court.

SPRITES

SPRITES ARE COLORFUL fairy spirits with shiny
wings. They mostly live in the deep woods
on branches of trees, and some of them reside
near ponds and streams. Sprites love to settle
in serene forests populated with other fairies.
They also travel in swarms and love pester-
ing butterflies—and bite if provoked. A tree
sprite will bathe in dew, while a ground or water
sprite may wash in ponds or rivers where it lives.

Sprites take care of the plants near their dwellings and often eat the pests that damage trees. Sprites are very similar to pixies but are much closer in appearance to insects than pixies are, and they live much closer to nature.

T

THUSSERS

THUSSERS ARE CREATURES from Norwegian folklore that are also known as Vardogls. They are small and live in earthen mounds. They come out at night to sing, dance, and party but are shy and flee at the approach of humans. A thusser is not malicious. In some stories, they are skilled metalworkers, which makes them distinct and strange, because metal is taboo to most fairies.

TINGOI

THE TINGOI IS a water spirit from the folklore of the Mende people of Sierra Leone. They are said to look mostly like young women with skin like a mermaid. They are extremely beautiful and preside over female initiation ceremonies. Stories and myths about the Tingoi are connected to the conceptions of beauty among the Mende. They are said to appear in dreams, for instance, as fulfillment of the erotic desires of both men and women, as part of the understanding that beauty is bound up in carnality, and not removed from the rest of human desire. Beyond sexual longing, the Tingoi are also sometimes the fulfillment of desires for wealth; leaving behind and sometimes taking away their comb in dreams is said to symbolize this. This understanding of the Tingoi as the complete reflection of beauty as it resides in the imagination has become inspiration for many artistic depictions, and stories about them continued to be shared into the twentieth and twenty-first centuries. While Tingoi are an ideal of beauty in its unattainable form, other conceptions of beauty among the Mende are Néku, which is the beauty that can be seen around us and in nature, and Haenjo, which is used to describe a person whose appearance approaches the culture's aesthetic standards.

TOKOLOSHE

TOKOLOSHES ARE TERRIFYING spirits from Zulu mythology in South Africa. They are very small, resembling either a primate or something more humanlike in appearance. They can become invisible by drinking water or eating a pebble. They are malicious and very dangerous, known to crawl into people's homes to scare them and even choke their victims to death. They enjoy

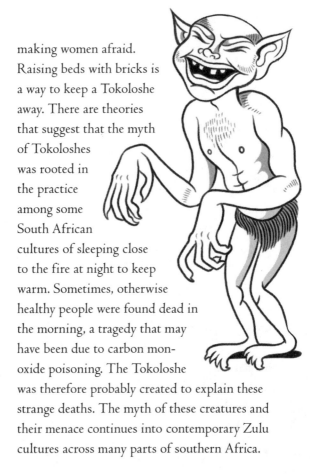

making women afraid.
Raising beds with bricks is
a way to keep a Tokoloshe
away. There are theories
that suggest that the myth
of Tokoloshes
was rooted in
the practice
among some
South African
cultures of sleeping close
to the fire at night to keep
warm. Sometimes, otherwise
healthy people were found dead in
the morning, a tragedy that may
have been due to carbon mon-
oxide poisoning. The Tokoloshe
was therefore probably created to explain these
strange deaths. The myth of these creatures and
their menace continues into contemporary Zulu
cultures across many parts of southern Africa.

U

UNDINE

UNDINES ARE ELEMENTAL spirits associated with water. Their name is derived from the Latin word *unda*, which means "wave." It was coined by Swiss renaissance alchemist Paracelsus, who was born Theophrastus von Hohenheim. These elemental spirits are often depicted as female, and in stories, men who fall in love with them die if they are ever unfaithful. Marriage to humans shortens the time undines can live in human form, but it earns them a soul. The off-spring of an undine and a human is usually a human with a soul and a characteristic called a watermark, for example, a portion of flesh that needs to be submerged in water periodically to prevent pain.

THE UNSEELIE COURT

THE UNSEELIE COURT is the fairy court of malicious and evil fairies, typically thought of as being the opposite of the **Seelie Court** (see page 108). Fairies in this court do not have to be offended to be evil toward humans. They move at night and attack ignorant people physically and mentally. They can sometimes be motivated to do good and offer help, but they are always more inclined toward evil.

URSITORY

THE MYTH OF the three female beings who ascribe fate to men are known in many cultures around the world. In Balkan and Romani folklore, these are the Ursitory, a group of three female fairies. Two of them are regarded as good spirits and one is known to try to hurt people.

According to the myths about them, they arrive on the third night after the birth of a baby to foretell the baby's fate. Only the baby can see them, but the mother and midwife can hear their words. The Ursitory became

well-known after the 1946 titular novel by
Matéo Maximoff, a French writer of Romani
origins. The Ursitory are still a part of Romani
folklore, as they have been for centuries.

V

VODYANOI

VODYANOI ARE WATER spirits from Slavic
mythology. In Czech and Slovak fairy tales,
they are called vodnik. A female vodyanoi is
also known as vodianikha. They live in lakes,
ponds, rivers, and other bodies of water. They
are humanlike but with big paws, horns, tails,
and burning eyes. Sometimes they look like a
huge man with shaggy fur; or like a half fish, half
human; or humpbacked with feet and the tail of

a cow. When they look like full humans, they can be identified by water coming out of their coats. They are immortal but grow younger and older with the moon. They are weak on land but powerful in the water and rest during the day so they can go out in the evenings. They are not usually hostile toward fishers and millers, and these people leave food like bread, salt, and vodka on the edge of the water as an offering for the vodyanoi. When they get angry, the vodyanoi break dams and water mills and drown people.

XANA

THE XANA ARE mythological creatures from Asturian mythology in northwest Spain. They are small and slender, with curls in their hair made with golden combs fashioned from sunbeams or moonbeams. A Xana can be a beneficial spirit but sometimes attacks travelers and steals their food. The Xana sing, and their voices can be heard on summer and spring nights—and the pure of heart will find peace in those voices while those with impure souls will be terrorized by the singing.

The Xana bear children called Xanin but cannot take care of them because of their inability to breastfeed their offspring. They swap their children with human babies so humans can raise their children, and humans often do not know about the change until a few months have passed. The babies can be made to

reveal themselves if the Xana put a pot of eggshells by the fire, which the Xanin cannot resist commenting aloud about. Some Xana suffer from a curse that they can be freed from in an obscure ritual.

YAKSHA

THE YAKSHA ARE creatures from Indian mythology in Hindu, Jain, and Buddhist texts. The female form of a Yaksha is a Yaksini. The Yaksha are depicted as big-bellied with small limbs and a big face with chubby cheeks, while Yaksini are portrayed as beautiful young women with happy, round faces. The Yaksha are known to have dual personalities: They can be benevolent nature spirits, but also a kind of ghost who haunts and attacks travelers. They are often given homage as the tutelary deities of a city, town, district, or lake. Belief in the Yaksha, along with other creatures such as the naga, are presumed to have originated among Indigenous people in India, and their worship is said have coincided with other religious practices of the Vedic period around 1500 BCE.

YEHASURI

YEHASURI ARE NATURE spirits from the folklore of the Catawba people in modern-day South Carolina, in the United States. The word *Yehasuri* means "not human ones" in Catawba. These little people are said to be hairy, dwarf-like tricksters whose acts of mischief can become very destructive. They can also be helpful, and they love singing, drumming, and dancing. They live in holes beneath trees and stumps and eat acorns, fungi, and tadpoles. It is believed that the only way to stop a Yehasuri is to rub tobacco on one's hand and recite an ancient Catawba prayer.

On the Catawba Nation reservation, there is a self-guided walk on an old wagon road called Yehasuri Trail, which leads to the Catawba River.

YŌSEI

THE YŌSEI ARE creatures of Japanese mythology who are said to attract ghosts. A yōsei is innocent, playful, and a little intelligent. They can learn to speak human languages and some are even said to have mastered sign language. Humans can only see them as birds, and they typically take the form of cranes and swans.

YUMBO

A YUMBO IS a creature from the mythology of the Wolof people in Senegal, specifically from south of the Cape Verde Peninsula. Yumboes are white-skinned, silver-haired spirits of the dead who stand about two feet tall. They are known to live in underground hills shaped like breasts that are a few miles off the coast, and they come out to dance in the moonlight and to sneak into nearby villages.

CONCLUSION

We've reached the end, but this little encyclopedia is only a sampling of all the fairies who exist in the world. May the fairies included here send you on your own magical journey to learning more and drawing your own conclusions about the role of the supernatural across cultures, time periods, and spiritual beliefs.

Hopefully this book encourages your own magical thinking. Fairies can bring good tidings or stir up trouble, but either way, they're known to effect change. If you're at some kind of cross-roads in your life and find yourself facing the unknown, let fairy magic in. Fairies have been known to favor those who call on them. Trust that these small yet powerful beings are there, filling in the gaps, doing work behind the scenes.

WORKS CITED

"Adama Delphine Fawundu/Tingoi." *Granary Arts.* Accessed
    May 15, 2023. https://www.granaryarts.org
    /adama-delphine-fawundu-tingoi.

Baker, Sidney J. "Origins of the Words Pakeha and Maori."
    Journal of the Polynesian Society 54, no. 4 (1945): 223–31.
    https://www.jps.auckland.ac.nz/document//Volume
    _54_1945/Volume_54%2C_No._4/Origins_of_
    the_words_Pakeha_and_Maori%2C_by_Sidney_J.
    _Baker%2C_p_223-231/p1.

Bane, Theresa. *Encyclopedia of Beasts and Monsters in Myth, Legend and
    Folklore.* Jefferson, NC: McFarland & Company, 2016.

Basu, Anindita. "Apsaras and Gandharvas." *World History
    Encyclopedia,* September 5, 2016. https://www
    .worldhistory.org/Apsaras_and_Gandharvas/.

Boone, Sylvia Ardyn. *Radiance from the Waters: Ideals of Feminine
    Beauty in Mende Art.* New Haven, CT: Yale University
    Press, 1986.

Callaway, Henry. *Nursery Tales, Traditions, and Histories of the
    Zulus: In Their Own Words, with a Translation into English and
    Notes,* Vol. 1. London: Trübner and Co., 1868. http://
    archive.org/details/nurserytalestra00callgoog.

Cartwright, Mark. "Leprechaun." *World History Encyclopedia,*
    February 4, 2021. https://www.worldhistory.org
    /Leprechaun/.

WORKS CITED

Craig, Robert D. *Dictionary of Polynesian Mythology.* Westport, CT: Greenwood Publishing Group, 1989.

"Dragon Species: Kaukas." *Circle of the Dragon.* Accessed May 15, 2023. https://www.blackdrago.com/species/kaukas.htm.

Editors of Encyclopaedia Britannica. "Khoekhoe." *Britannica.* Updated October 5, 2021. https://www.britannica.com/topic/Khoekhoe.

———. "Lauma." *Britannica.* Updated September 10, 2020. https://www.britannica.com/topic/lauma.

———. "Yaksha." *Britannica.* Updated February 27, 2023. https://www.britannica.com/topic/yaksha.

Edwards, Eric. "The Pixie." *Eric Edwards Collected Works* (blog), November 28, 2013. https://ericwedwards.wordpress.com/2013/11/28/the-pixie/.

Ettachfini, Leila. "What Are Jinn: The Arab Spirits Who Can Eat, Sleep, Have Sex, and Die." *Vice,* October 31, 2018. https://www.vice.com/en/article/9k7ekv/what-are-jinn-arab-spirits.

Evans, Ivor H. N. *Studies in Religion, Folk-Lore, & Custom in British North Borneo and the Malay Peninsula.* London: Routledge, 1923.

Field, M. J. "The Asamanukpai of the Gold Coast." *Man* 34, no. 211 (December 1934): 186–89. https://doi.org/10.2307/2790338.

"The Fomorians: Destructive Giants of Irish Legend." *Ancient Origins.* Updated December 28, 2017. https://

www.ancient-origins.net/myths-legends-europe
/fomorians-destructive-giants-irish-legend-009349.

Fuchs, Brigitte. "'Bushmen in Hick Town': The Austrian
Empire and the Study of the Khoesan." *Austrian
Studies* 20 (2012): 43–59. https://doi.org/10.5699
/austrianstudies.20.2012.0043.

Gill, N. S. "Who Are the Nymphs in Greek Mythology?"
ThoughtCo. Updated May 28, 2019. https://www
.thoughtco.com/nymphs-in-greek-mythology-118497.

Johncock, Graeme. "The Baobhan Sith." *Folklore Scotland.*
Accessed May 15, 2023. https://folklorescotland
.com/the-baobhan-sith/.

Keightley, Thomas. *The Fairy Mythology.* London: W. H.
Ainsworth, 1828.

———. *The Fairy Mythology: Illustrative of the Romance and
Superstition of Various Countries.* London: H. G. Bohn, 1850.

Largo, Jim. "Catawba Little People Picked on Children."
ICT News, September 12, 2018. https://ictnews.org
/archive/catawba-little-people-picked-on-children.

"Lauma (mythology)." *Heroes Wiki.* Accessed May 15, 2023.
https://hero.fandom.com/wiki/Lauma_(mythology).

Lombardi, Linda. "Kappa: Japan's Aquatic, Cucumber-
Loving, Booty-Obsessed Yokai." *Tofugu,* June 16, 2015.
https://www.tofugu.com/japan/kappa/.

Mark, Joshua J. "Kikimora." *World History Encyclopedia.*
October 11, 2021. https://www.worldhistory.org
/Kikimora/.

Martin, Paula, and Margaret Read MacDonald. *Pachamama Tales: Folklore from Argentina, Bolivia, Chile, Paraguay, Peru, and Uruguay.* Santa Barbara, CA: Libraries Unlimited, 2014.

"May 11th & the Lunantishees." *Crimson Sage* (blog). May 11, 2021. https://crimsonsageaz.com// post/1037959135601/may-11th-the-lunantishees.

McCoy, Edain. *A Witch's Guide to Faery Folk: Reclaiming Our Working Relationship with Invisible Helpers.* Saint Paul, MN: Llewellyn Worldwide, 1994.

"Mokumokuren." *Wikipedia.* Last modified March 8, 2023. https://en.wikipedia.org/w/index.php?title= Mokumokuren&oldid=1143561595.

Murillo Argandoña, Adriana L. Translated by Niall Flynn. "The Achachilas." *Bolivian Express Magazine,* March 26, 2018. https://bolivianexpress.org/blog/posts/the-achachilas.

New World Encyclopedia contributors. "Gandharva." *New World Encyclopedia.* Last modified April 2, 2008. https:// www.newworldencyclopedia.org/entry/Gandharva.

"Nisse (folklore)." *Wikipedia.* Last modified May 9, 2023. https://en.wikipedia.org/w/index.php?title=Nisse_ (folklore)&oldid=1153996278.

"Nuku-mai-tore." *Encyclopedia Mythica,* October 13, 2006. https://pantheon.org/articles/n/nuku-mai-tore.html.

"Nykr." *Myths and Folklore Wiki.* Accessed May 15, 2023. https://mythus.fandom.com/wiki/Nykr.

Pires, Rogério Brittes W., Stuart Earle Strange, and Marcelo Moura Mello. "The Bakru Speaks: Money-Making

WORKS CITED

Demons and Racial Stereotypes in Guyana and Suriname." *New West Indian Guide / Nieuwe West-Indische Gids* 92, no. 1–2 (May 1, 2018): 1–34. https://doi.org/10.1163/22134360-09201001.

Pursiful, Darrell J. "Jogaoh: Iroquois Fair Folk." *Darrell J. Pursiful,* January 17, 2014. https://pursiful.com/2014/01/17/jogaoh-iroquois-fair-folk/.

Reynolds, June. "Gremlins: A Nineteenth Century Mythology." *Medium,* November 24, 2019. https://medium.com/@junereynolds/gremlins-a-nineteenth-century-mythology-c0254c605db9.

Rogers, Charles, and Grampian Club. *Scotland, Social and Domestic: Memorials of Life and Manners in North Britain.* London: Grampian Club, 1869.

Sallustio, Michael. "Huldufólk: The Truth behind Iceland's Obsession with Elves." *The Portalist,* December 21, 2018. https://theportalist.com/huldufolk-the-truth-behind-icelands-obsession-with-elves.

Scott, Walter. *Letters on Demonology and Witchcraft.* London: J. & J. Harper, 1830.

"The Seelie Court." *The Faire Folk* (blog). Accessed May 15, 2023. https://thefairefolk-rp.tumblr.com/theseeliecourt.

"Sprites." *Mythical Creatures Guide.* Accessed May 15, 2023. https://www.mythicalcreaturesguide.com/sprites/.

Studarus, Laura. "The Elusive 'Hidden People' of Iceland." BBC, December 18, 2018. https://www.bbc.com/travel/article/20181217-the-elusive-hidden-people-of-iceland.

WORKS CITED

"Those with Feet-in-Reverse and Other Fantastical Beings." *Cultures of West Africa* (blog), July 29, 2019. https://www.culturesofwestafrica.com/feet-in-reverse-fantastical-beings/.

"The Tokoloshe." *Astonishing Legends* (blog). February 16, 2019. https://www.astonishinglegends.com/astonishing-legends/2019/2/16/the-tokoloshe.

van der Veen, Abe J. "Elfenbedrog En Elfenwaarheid." *Abe de Verteller.* Accessed May 15, 2023. https://www.abedeverteller.nl/elfenbedrog-en-elfenwaarheid/.

Viking Roots. "Tomte (the ancestor spirit)." Facebook, December 31, 2015. https://www.facebook.com/235623266577320/photos/a.235682906571356/649550041851305.

"Vodyanoi." *A Book of Creatures,* December 21, 2015. https://abookofcreatures.com/2015/12/21/vodyanoi/.

"Xana." *Myths and Folklore Wiki.* Accessed May 15, 2023. https://mythus.fandom.com/wiki/Xana.

"Yosei." *Wikipedia.* Last modified April 8, 2023. https://en.wikipedia.org/w/index.php?title=Y%C5%8Dsei&oldid=1148828399.

INDEX

INDEX

INDEX

ABOUT THE AUTHOR

OJO OPANIKE is a writer from Ogbomoso, Nigeria, living in Atlanta, Georgia. He writes short stories and essays on Nigerian music and visual arts and spends all his time thinking about masquerades.

ABOUT THE ILLUSTRATOR

KATE FORRESTER is a freelance illustrator from the south coast of England. She specializes in creating bespoke hand-lettering and intricate illustrations for book covers, packaging, and many other applications. More than anything, Kate loves telling stories and collaborating with her clients and authors to bring their words to life.